Contents

puppet show

Once you have finished making one puppet, you won't be able to stop! Ask all your friends and family to join in and soon you will have enough puppets to put on a show.

1 To make a bird puppet, find two round boxes, one slightly larger than the other. You'll also need some coloured paper, feathers, beads and a length of dowel about 25cm long.

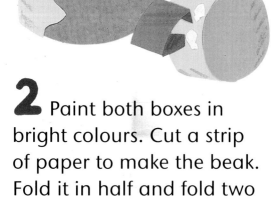

2 Paint both boxes in bright colours. Cut a strip of paper to make the beak. Fold it in half and fold two small flaps at either end. Glue the flaps in place on the smaller box.

let's make
Toys

Ivan Bulloch & Diane James

Created by
Two-Can Publishing Ltd
346 Old Street
London EC1V 9NQ

Art Director Ivan Bulloch
Editor Diane James
Illustrator Emily Hare
Photographer Daniel Pangbourne
Models Kaz, Kerri, Rahmel, Ben, Alesha, Mathew, Rio,

First published by Two-Can Publishing Ltd in 1997
in association with Franklin Watts

Hardback ISBN 1-85434-516-8
Paperback ISBN 1-85434-518-4

Dewey Decimal Classification 745.592

Paperback 2 4 6 8 10 9 7 5 3

A catalogue record for this book is available from the British Library

Printed in Spain by Graficromo S.A

just you listen to me!

tweet, tweet

tweet!

3 Ask a grown-up to make a hole in the large box, big enough to slot the dowel through. This will be the handle for you to operate your puppet.

4 Glue the boxes together and stick on the feathers, paper wings and bead eyes. Push the dowel up into the hole in the large box. What can you make your bird puppet do?

bowl them over

Here's a great game to enjoy with your friends, or on your own. It won't take you long to make and you can play it over and over again. Write the scores on a piece of paper. The winner is the person to knock the most bottles over after a certain number of goes.

let's get started!

1 Collect six empty plastic bottles, the same size. Make sure they are clean and dry. Don't use glass bottles because they may break. Cut strips of coloured paper to fit round the bottles.

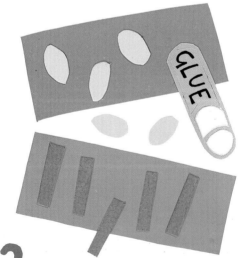

2 Cut or tear shapes from coloured paper and glue them on to decorate the paper strips.

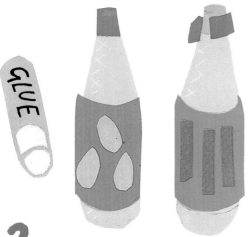

GLUE

3 Wrap a decorated strip round each bottle and glue or tape it in place. Glue another narrow strip of paper round the top.

4 Arrange the bottles in a triangle. Stand about three metres away. Roll a soft ball, aiming for the single bottle in the centre. Count the bottles you knock over and set them up again for a friend to try.

the champion!

beat it out!

Have you ever thought of starting a band? The first instrument you'll need is a noisy drum! Make one just like the one here and you will soon be entertaining all your friends!

1 We used a plastic waste-paper basket to make our drum. A cake tin or plastic container also works. Stand the waste-paper basket upside down on a large sheet of greaseproof paper and draw round the outside.

3 Stand your drum upright. Put the circle of paper on top. Fold the triangles over the edge and use small pieces of tape to keep the paper firmly in place. Stretch it as tight as possible but don't tear it!

2 Draw another circle about 5cm outside the first one. Cut the circle out carefully, around the outside edge. Ask a grown-up to help you cut small triangle shapes between the two circles. The drawing shows you how to do this.

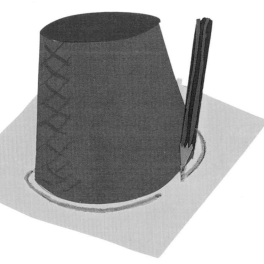

4 Wind a length of sticky tape round the top of the drum. Decorate the drum by gluing on shapes cut from coloured paper.

8

rat-a-tat!

boom, boom!

5 Wooden spoons make terrific drum sticks! You can decorate them by winding coloured sticky tape round the handles. Don't bang too hard, use your sticks gently.

play with me

This is a game to play outdoors when the sun is shining, or indoors when it's cold and wet. You won't need any sand if you are playing inside! Concentrate hard, and no cheating!

1 Look out for sticks or twigs to make the grid for your game. You will also need 10 stones for the pieces to play with.

2 Make sure the stones are clean and dry. Paint a bright background colour on each one. When the paint is dry, add crosses to five of the stones and circles, or noughts, to the other five.

3 Lay the sticks on the ground, using the picture below as a guide.

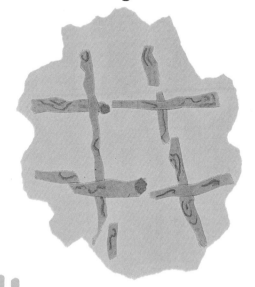

4 Each player takes five stones. One has all the crosses, the other has the noughts. Take it in turn to put a stone in a square. The winner is the first to make a line with their stones.

11

animal fun

It may look messy, but working with salt dough is great fun and you can make all sorts of things. Try making your own zoo or farm animals, or some friendly pets to play with!

1 Tip two mugs of flour, one mug of salt and one mug of water into a large mixing bowl.

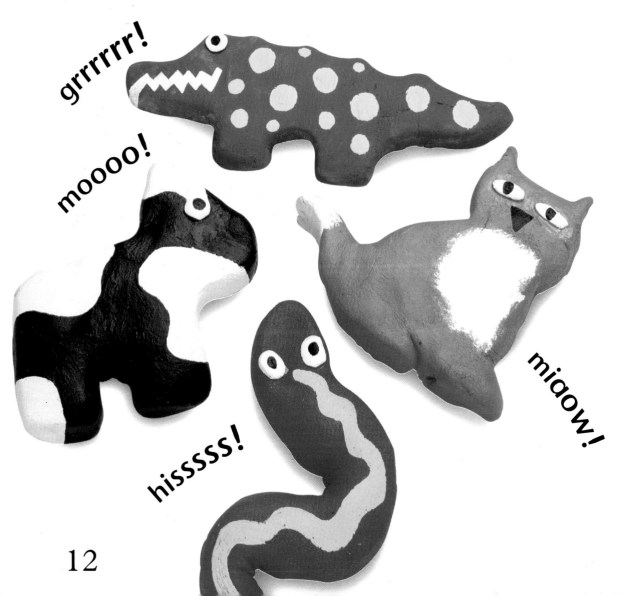

grrrrrr!

mooooo!

hisssss!

miaow!

2 Mix everything together well with your hands. Bring the mixture together into a large ball and knead it well until the dough is smooth and firm.

sticky fingers!

3 Pull off pieces of dough and model them into shapes. Keep the shapes simple, and not too thick. Put them on a baking tray.

4 Ask a grown-up to heat the oven to 130°C, (250°F, gas mark 1/2). Put your shapes in the oven for about one hour. Very thick shapes will take a little longer. Ask a grown-up to take them out of the oven. When the shapes are cold, you can paint them.

splish, splash!

You can be captain of your very own fleet of boats! Make some sponge boats, just like the ones here, and you can be sure that they will never sink! How many boats do you think you can fit in your bath?

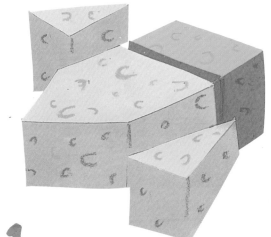

1 Start with two chunky sponges to make a base for your boat. Cut a pointed end in one of them. Ask a grown-up to help with the cutting.

2 Cut two strips from a thin sponge dishcloth to make funnels. Roll them up and glue down the ends. Use a waterproof glue and ask a grown-up to read the instructions on the tube.

ahoy there!

GLUE

3 Glue the base shapes together. When the glue is dry, stick on a bath sponge with rounded ends. Wait for the glue to dry and stick on the funnels. Just a few more minutes and your boat will be ready to sail! Now try making a different boat.

4 For an instant boat, cut a chunky sponge shape like the one above. Ask a grown-up to make two slits in the top. Push a funnel into the slits. The sponge will spring back and grip the funnel in place.

knock, knock!

Is your bedroom a bit crowded? Would you like to have a whole house to yourself? With a little bit of help *and* a big, empty box, there will be enough room for you inside and a friendly visitor can join you, too!

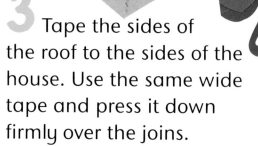

3 Tape the sides of the roof to the sides of the house. Use the same wide tape and press it down firmly over the joins.

1 Find a huge cardboard box. Department stores selling fridges and cookers may have one to spare. Ask a grown-up to help you cut off the bottom, and cut out a door and window.

2 Tape two large sheets of cardboard together to make a roof to fit the top of your house. Use wide tape on both sides of the join to make it strong.

4 Paint your house and roof in your favourite colours, or leave the walls unpainted to look more natural. Don't forget the window and door frame!

16

special delivery for you!

5 Now it's time for the garden! Cut some grass and flowers from coloured paper and glue them round the bottom of your house.

17

cuddly bunny

How many fluffy, furry, cuddly creatures have you got? Probably at least one teddy bear! If you want to add to your family, or give someone a special present, try making a funny bunny like the one here.

1 Cut two squares of felt, roughly the size of the toy you want to make. We decided on a bunny! Use a crayon or a piece of chalk to draw a shape on the top piece of felt.

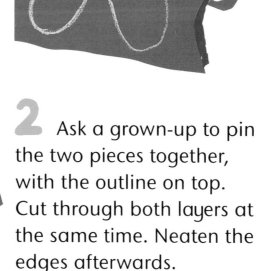

2 Ask a grown-up to pin the two pieces together, with the outline on top. Cut through both layers at the same time. Neaten the edges afterwards.

3 Take the top shape of felt and give your bunny a face! Ask a grown-up to help you sew on large coloured buttons for eyes. Glue on felt shapes to make a nose, mouth and paws. Add a big felt bow tie.

4 Now, with a bit more help, you can sew the two pieces of your bunny together. Use some coloured wool and a needle with a big eye. Try to make your stitches evenly spaced.

5 When you have stitched almost all the way round your bunny, stop! Leave a gap of about 4cm. To make the stuffing, chop some old tights into small pieces. Push them into the gap and pad out the ears, paws, legs and tummy. Stitch up the gap neatly and fasten off the end of the wool.

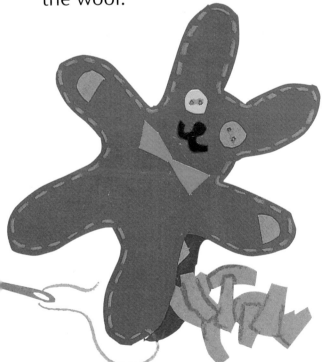

drive in

Have you got a collection of cars? Why not make a multi-level garage for them. As well as being fun to play with, it is a good way to keep your cars together in one place.

1 Ask a grown-up to help you cut three pieces of card to the measurements shown on the drawing.

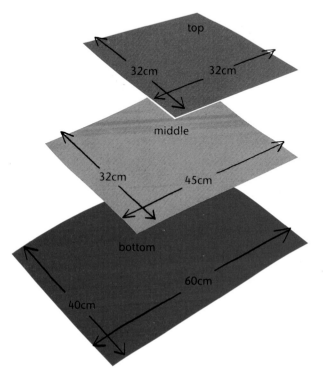

top
32cm 32cm
middle
32cm 45cm
bottom
60cm
40cm

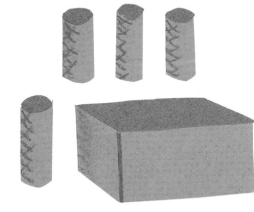

2 You will also need four cardboard tubes and two small cardboard boxes 12cm high.

3 To make the ramps, ask for some help to cut slits in the middle and top floors of your garage. Use the measurements shown. Score along the top edge of the ramp and fold it downwards.

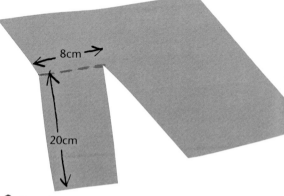

8cm
20cm

4 Paint all the garage parts. Add arrows to show the cars which way to go! When the paint is dry, you can start putting your garage together.

beep! beep!

5 Lay the base on the floor. Using the picture as a guide, add a small box and two tubes. Place the middle level on top. Add another box and two more tubes. Now you can put the top level on. Glue the parts in place as you go, so your garage doesn't fall to pieces when you play with it!

vroom, vroom!

Here's a car that goes without petrol and if you drive it carefully it will last for ages! Perhaps you would like to turn your car into an ambulance, a fire engine, or a speedy police car?

2 Paint the outside of the box including the lip at the top. Add patterns using coloured paper.

1 Look out for a large cardboard box, big enough to fit over your head and body! Ask a grown-up to cut out the bottom and top, leaving a lip at the top where you can attach the straps.

3 Glue on tin foil dishes for headlights and a plastic container to look like a radiator. Can you think of anything else? A paper plate makes a perfect steering wheel!

here I come!

look out!

4 Ask a grown-up to make two slits at both sides of your car on the lip of card. The slits should be long enough to slot lengths of wide ribbon through.

5 You will need help with this bit! Poke lengths of ribbon through the front slits, criss-cross them over and poke them through the back slits. Put the car on and adjust the length of the ribbons. Make knots in the ends of the ribbons.

tips and tricks

Here are some of our favourite tips to help you become a top-class toy maker!

1 Keep a collection of all sorts of bits and pieces. Save boxes, coloured paper, ribbons, feathers, beads, pebbles and shells.

2 Look at toys and games in toy shops and magazines to get ideas for making your own. Don't try anything too complicated!

3 Ask your friends to join in and help. This will speed things up! And they can play with you when the toy or game is finished.

4 When you are painting, always spread newspaper or polythene on the working surface.

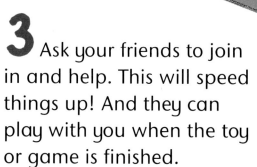

5 Wash your paint brushes in cold water when you have finished.